WE ARE OVERCOME

When Malcolm X said "equality would be achieved by any means necessary," was he anticipating the 1995 birth rate for fourteen-year-old black girls?

When Stokeley declared "Black Power!" in 1966, do you think Clarence Thomas was what he had in mind?

Well, neither does Bonnie Allen, the first black female political/social humorist, who dissects blacks *and* whites in her provocative, irreverent, outspoken, and highly anticipated book of original essays. *We Are Overcome* tries to make sense out of the last quarter-century in black American life. What P. J. O'Rourke does for Right-thinking people and Molly Ivins does for Texas politics, Bonnie Allen will do for people everywhere who are trying to get a handle on that slippery oxymoron, race relations.

Groundbreaking and insightful, *We Are Overcome* examines the actions and attitudes rearing up in America since that warm, fuzzy "civil rights movement" *moment* in history when blacks and whites marched arm-in-arm through the streets of our nation, blending their voices in a soul-wrenching medley of "Kumbaya" and "Go Down Moses," and seeking a better world with equal opportunities for all on a *somewhat* level playing field. Unfortunately, white America didn't reveal that equal opportunities were only available

(continued on back flap)

WE ARE OVERCOME

Thoughts on Being Black in America

BONNIE ALLEN

Crown Publishers, Inc.
New York

Published by Crown Publishers, Inc., 201 East 50th Street,
New York, New York 10022. Member of the Crown Pub-
lishing Group.

Random House, Inc. New York, Toronto, London, Sydney,
Auckland

CROWN is a trademark of Crown Publishers, Inc.

Manufactured in the United States of America

Design by Lauren Dong

Library of Congress Cataloging-in-Publication Data
Allen, Bonnie.
    We are overcome: thoughts on being Black in
America / by Bonnie Allen.—1st. ed.
    1. United States—Race relations.   2. United
States—Race relations—Humor.   3. Afro-Americans—
Social conditions—1975-   4. Afro-Americans—Social
conditions—1975- —Humor.   I. Title.
E185.615.A63   1995
305.8'00973—dc20   95-5141
                                              CIP

ISBN 0-517-59759-4

10   9   8   7   6   5   4   3   2   1

First Edition

For Darryl Minger,

who should have been here.

Contents

Acknowledgments

*I*f I thanked everyone who made it possible for me to write this book, this page would read like one of those run-on Academy Awards acceptance speeches that make audiences start flipping channels to see if anything exciting is happening on *Baywatch*. So I'll just skip my cats and go with the short list.

There's Myrna Bers, who's been my best friend for thirty years, no matter how hard I try, and Marcella Lowery, who read this manuscript and bought me a bulletproof vest. Thanks to Maybelle and Ernie Allen for creating the last functional family in America fifty-four years ago and for having so much stability that I didn't need any. Ditto their two sons, Ernie and Doug, for their critical eyes (one apiece).

In alphabetical order, I wouldn't be here without the friendship, intellectual support, and/or

ACKNOWLEDGMENTS

child-care services of Anita Edwards, Thelma Hudgins, Janet Lenter, Angelina May, Jacqueline Perry, Geoffrey Pete, LaTanya Richardson, Danni Tyson, and Cheryl Wilson.

Great appreciation to my editor, Carol Taylor; my agent, Marlene Connor; and my daughter, Paloma Allen-Davis, who knows how (and when) to make me laugh, and how to come through when I need her. And also to my fellow faculty members at Peaches' School of Charm and Negro Improvement—you know who you are.

The mind is a terrible thing to waste.

—THE UNITED NEGRO COLLEGE FUND

WE ARE OVERCOME

Introduction

When I was growing up in Oakland, California, in the fifties and sixties, being an African-American was a simple issue. Neighborhoods were redlined. Employment was segregated. Banks discriminated. You never asked a police officer for assistance, for fear of death and dismemberment. Other than that, you were free. God bless America.

I've been trying to put my finger on when the racial situation got a little more complicated. It seems like it was sometime after Kunta Kinte discovered America but before Lee Atwater discovered Willie Horton. One minute we were all holding hands, Blacks and whites together, overcoming and what all. The next thing I know, the melanin-impaired segment of the population is signing a contract asking Newt Gingrich to erase the Congressional Black Caucus from the face of the earth and turn back the clock to the good old days of Ike, Doris Day, Pat Boone, Amos, Andy, and Beulah. (Please note: I have seen the good old days, and once was more than enough. I do not do windows.)

There are many ways to approach the question of how we moved from the back of the bus to the back of the national priority list in just one generation. If I was an academic, I would probably do it with a heavily footnoted, fact-filled, thoroughly detailed tome. Fortunately for you, nobody's ever accused me of being an academic.

I am taking a completely different tack to look at who we are and how we got to where we are (particularly since, on many levels, we hadn't planned to pass this way again). If after reading this book you still feel a niggling urge for more facts, more concrete data, more *just plain information*, go out and volunteer at a homeless shelter. Obviously, you have been floating too close to the glass ceiling and you need to get a quick blast of humanity before you tip over the edge.

As for what really happened to Black America in the last thirty years, here's a thought: In 1969, on a wet and dreary summer afternoon, I was walking down a street in Harlem. Rain had been coming down for so many days, it was as if God's drainpipes had backed up and overflowed. Too much rain for summer. Absolutely, unquestionably, unnatural rain.

An old lady, the kind who would find herself homeless in another decade, stood in front of me on the street. She looked up at the waterlogged heavens, peered through the drops, and said, "I told them white men they should have never walked on the moon."

Maybe she was onto something.

How Do You Guarantee the Black Vote in '96?

(Hint: Don't Ask Ed Rollins.)

*F*ar be it from me to generalize, but it seems that Republican presidential candidates have never had much of a knack for capturing the hearts and minds of African-American voters. Maybe it's because the white men on the GOP ticket often appear to carry an indefinable aura . . . a special something that proclaims, without having to state it, I've never, ever touched a Black person by choice (Pearl Bailey and Sammy Davis, Jr., do not count here).

This is probably not a completely accurate characterization. More likely, a perception problem exists, resulting from the fact that these candidates had no African-American peers during their formative years. They simply didn't have the advantage of just one Black friend who could look them in the eye and say, Hey, my family's not on welfare, I don't carry a gun, and it wouldn't occur to me to rape your sister.

Think of it this way: Did the young George Bush ever venture out of his restricted neighborhood to share a squash game with a hail-fellow-well-met, rep tie–wearing, "Boola Boola"–singing Negro? Less than likely. Did Dan Quayle ever try to integrate either his fraternity or his golf course? Did Ronald Reagan ever party with Stepin Fetchit during their glory years in Hollywood? The answers speak for themselves.

Fortunately for Republicans, there are still

enough white people left in America to deliver an election. Republicans can get along fine without the Black vote as long as their basic party platform appeals to those with a fervid desire to maintain what's left of the privilege of being white, and who display a pronounced fear of:

- crime (aka unincarcerated Black youth)
- uterine autonomy
- gay pride
- non-God-fearing-fundamentalist-Judeo-Christians
- aliens (aka immigrants from Black, Latino, and queer nations)
- uppity women
- Democrats
- anyone defined as "other"

The Democratic party is not so lucky. When African-American voters don't come out strongly for a Democrat, he's got as much of a chance of winning as Herb Stempel in *Quiz Show*. Just ask David Dinkins. Unless the Democratic party wants Bill Clinton to become the Vanilla Ice of presidential politics, they must begin immediately to search out new and exciting ways of attracting African-American voters.

The good news is that even though not one government promise has been fulfilled since that "forty acres and a mule" debacle, Black people still, on occasion, vote. And for some odd reason, they still vote overwhelmingly Democratic. Why? you might reasonably ask. According to Rush Limbaugh and his posse of listeners, it's because every African-American in America, with the exception of Oprah, collects a welfare check from bleeding-heart liberal Democrats. Not so. Democrats have not, in fact, been liberal for years.

Rather, it's a question of instinct—some intangible feeling that the Democratic candidate (with the mutant exception of Michael Dukakis) is not personally offended by the fact that your ilk is taking up space on the planet. It probably goes back to that aforementioned "touch" thing.

For instance, Franklin Roosevelt did not touch Black people on a daily basis, but his wife did. Harry Truman integrated the armed services, making it possible for thousands of African-Americans to die alongside their red-necked brethren. JFK touched more Black women than we'd care to know about. Okay, nobody touched LBJ if they could help it, but Jimmy Carter had African-American friends even before it became politically astute to do so. Of course, so did Bill Clinton. Ask Lani Guinier.

In the fifties, this predisposed affinity, along with a couple of photo ops in *Jet* and *Ebony*, preferably standing next to Eleanor Roosevelt, would have been enough to guarantee a landslide victory among Black voters. As it stands, however, Mrs. Roosevelt is currently dead and appears to have forgotten to train a replacement. Bill Clinton offers no particular appeal to LaTiesha and Malik Q. Public. Whenever Democrats need to prove they're not "caving in to special interests," they publicly dis Jesse Jackson. All of this creates something of an image problem that will reverberate in the voting booth.

Which leads us to the one quick fix for '96: An African-American must be on the ticket. Not just *any* African-American. One with the intellectual capacity of W. E. B. Du Bois and the charm of Magic Johnson; the communication skills of Bryant Gumbel and the political savvy of Harold Washington. God, if Black and available, would certainly fill the bill. Otherwise, we should consider the following criteria:

1. He must be acceptable to white Americans. *This goes without saying.*

2. He must be a "he." *Ditto.*

3. He must not have been photographed hugging Louis Farrakhan, Leonard Jeffries, Khalid Muhammed, Chuck D, or Richard Nixon.

4. The following words should not ever have been used in a sentence containing his name:
   sexist
   sexual predator
   sexual harasser
   oversexed

5. He should never have been spotted wearing a T-shirt saying:

> IT'S A BLACK THING—YOU WOULDN'T UNDERSTAND
>
> FREE MIKE TYSON, CLARENCE THOMAS, AND STEDMAN
>
> LET THE JUICE LOOSE
>
> THE BITCH SET HIM UP

The tricky part is finding someone to satisfy the first criterion. When white people really, *really* like an African-American, odds are Blacks are going to think that person is a jerk—or not hot, at the very least. For this very reason, we can eliminate the following obvious, but ethnically unappealing, suggestions for the Democratic ticket in '96:

> Colin Powell
> M. C. Hammer
> Jimmie "J. J." Walker
> Doug Wilder
> George Jefferson
> Clarence Thomas
> O. J. Simpson
> Diana Ross

You may think this leaves us with no available candidate. Well, let us not forget Bill Cosby.

White America pretended to like him a lot back in the eighties, at least until he made more money than could possibly be encompassed by a Negro's proper place. There's also Michael Jordan, but the job requirements would probably interfere with his batting practice. Besides, neither of these men has the necessary *political* credentials. This is a job for a leader, someone who has proven he can tell his people where to go and how to get there.

Which brings us to a pair of candidates guaranteed to electrify every single Black voter in America. Yes, we're talking presidential *and* vice presidential candidates—an all-African-American ticket that provides more pizzazz than Bill Clinton, Dan Quayle, Edward Bennett, Newt Gingrich, Bob Dole, Jack Kemp, and Pat Robertson put together (not that this is a very difficult task). This is a ticket that will leave the press gasping in wonder and damn near speechless, which is not necessarily a bad thing. This is a totally balanced ticket, geographically and philosophically, with candidates who have achieved unprecedented support from worldwide religious organizations; human-rights groups; city, state, and national governments; rock groups; rappers; feminists; the Nation of Islam; the Hollywood film community; Middle America; the inner city; and, reluctantly, George Bush.

Yes, we are talking about Nelson Mandela for President, with Al Sharpton as his running mate.

The possibilities are awe-inspiring.

Of course the nattering nabobs of negativity will mention that Mr. Mandela is not exactly a native of the United States. Neither is Henry Kissinger, and that didn't stop him from running the country. Besides, does anyone besides Robert Bork really know what the Founding Fathers meant when they wrote the Constitution? Did they actually intend to take the Proposition 187 route and discriminate against the foreign-born? I think not. The Constitution is a living, ever-expanding document. If it weren't, African-Americans couldn't vote. (And by the way, while it is true Mr. Mandela has had a First Lady problem, so did Gerald Ford, and she turned out to be a credit to her race.)

As for Mr. Sharpton, so what if he's controversial? Dan Quayle, Ross Perot, and Pat Robertson have shown us that controversy brings out the activism in the committed voter. Besides, as we learned from Marion Barry, Black voters have a special affection for candidates who scare the hell out of white people. Democrat-bashers in the press may get hung up on Sharpton's unfortunate stint as an FBI informant, his Don King connection, and his curious handling of the mysterious Tawana Brawley incident. But that kind of press persecution didn't stop Ollie North from running, and it won't stop our Al.

There really is only one way to look at this scenario: Thelma and Louise at the Grand Canyon had more options than the Democrats in '96. But just as African-American voters saved the country from Ollie North, they can save it from itself. Otherwise, get ready for the cackling sounds of President Newt and his Armageddon agenda arriving just in time for the millennium.

Bill Clinton? His credibility in the African-American community is about as valid as Kenny G's jazz credentials. With Clinton's support of the "build more prisons to house potential African-American criminals until we kill them with the death penalty" crime bill, with his health care bill screwup, with his allowing Cubans to be designated political refugees while fleeing Haitians were packed away in crypto–concentration camps, Clinton will never be a motivating inspiration to Black voters. We have to go with the alternative:

From the Motherland to the Brotherland
Nelson & Al in '96

Jesse Jackson is available to give the nominating speech.

For Whom
the Bell
Curves

Dr. Charles Murray
Harvard University

Dear Dr. Murray,

I tried to read your best-seller, *The Bell Curve*, because, even though all the really important books have been written by dead white men and you're unfortunately not yet a member of that category, I thought you might have something meaningful to say. I found it rather perplexing. It seems your book is telling me that if IQ's are placed on a bell curve, then those of my ilk are the ding-a-lings.

I would be much obliged if you would answer the following questions to clear up my confusion, preferably using simple sentences and avoiding sesquipedalian vocabulary. (I am only, after all, a genetically IQ-impaired African-American and therefore am frequently addled by big ideas and big words.)

What I need to know

Is this genetically based IQ-impairment thing a purely African affliction, or did it occur when Africans were force-melted into the "American" DNA pot?

Is one drop of Black blood enough to afflict you, or does genetically based IQ-impairment apply only to the visibly melanined?

Speaking hypothetically of course, if Toni Morrison and Senator Alphonse D'Amato produce an offspring, would this improve the Black race?

If an African-American does not gain admittance to MENSA, may a claim be filed under the Americans with Disabilities Act?

Are light-skinned African-Americans more intelligent than darker-skinned African-Americans due to the increased white genetic material in their makeup? (As a follow-up: Would you be willing to state your answer onstage at a Public Enemy concert?)

Does being on the wrong end of the bell curve qualify as a handicapping condition, allowing one to take the SAT under special circumstances?

Does being on the wrong end of the bell curve qualify as a handicapping condition, allowing one to collect SSI or other exciting entitlements?

When white, corn-fed midwestern teenage females dress like Brooklyn hoochies, are they putting themselves at risk (speaking IQ-wise, of course)?

Have Harvard and Yale already established a quota for the genetically IQ-impaired, or should I wait to apply? To follow up: If I identify myself as biracial rather than African-American on a college application, will I still qualify?

How do quadroons fair, on an average? Octoroons? Sexdecadroons?

Is there any way of determining whether I was born with a genetically based IQ-impairment or if I am just dumb?

Genetically, eugenically, phrenologically, and social-scientifically speaking, what *are* African-Americans and when did they become a homogeneous race with equal genetic traits that could be objectively quantified?

Just wondering,
BONNIE ALLEN

Bootstrapping for Fun and Profit

The Black

Conservative Guide

bootstrapping\v.[nonstndrd/Afr Am slng/Blklish]1: the Booker T. Washington program through which uplifted colored people gained independence via self-help (i.e., "pulling oneself up by one's own bootstraps") 2: a physically challenging act of illusion requiring that you pull yourself up by the strap of your boots although Reaganomics, Bush-whacking, and Newtzi-ism have left you barefoot 3: the amazing art of African-Americans achieving success without the aid of the EEOC or the Justice Department 4: often synonymous with *bootlicking* (see *Samuel Pierce; Clarence Thomas*).

*B*ored with your job as affirmative-action manager for a company that doesn't believe in affirmative action? Tired of functioning as minority admissions adviser to a university with no minority enrollment? Welfare check just not making ends meet? Well, brother and/or sister, becoming an Amway distributor is no longer the only way out of your occupational doldrums. If you're ready to give up reliance on government quotas and set-asides, ready to denounce affirmative action and welfare dependence, ready to pick yourself up by your own bootstraps and take advantage of the opportunities available to *all* American citizens regardless of race, color, or creed, then we have an answer for you. Recently an exciting and rewarding career opportunity has opened up for up-and-coming neo-Negroes like yourself in the glamorous field of Black Conservative Spokesperson.

But am I qualified to be a spokesperson for Black America? As has been frequently demonstrated, experience and/or credentials are not a job requirement. As a matter of fact, all you need to compete successfully as a Black Conservative Spokesperson is the ability to speak out forcefully against entrenched social policies that discriminate against you as much as they do against the beleaguered white majority. If you can just explain to Your People the advantages of putting America first rather than wallowing in divisive issues such as race, if you can convince them to cast aside their infantile need for Big Brother and replace it with the good old-fashioned color-blind Puritan work ethic, you've got all of the qualifications you need.

By now, you're probably thinking to yourself, *is this going to cost me as much as one of those real estate infomercial seminars where I have to pay to earn?* Here's the good news: There's no money down and no monthly payments to obtain this fabulous position. In fact, prestigious Ivy League schools like Yale University offer reverse-discriminatory minority scholarships to pay you while you learn. What's more, by bootstrapping your way out of your present miserable condition and catapulting yourself into the action-packed arena of Black Conservative Spokesperson, you guarantee yourself a six-figure income from book sales, speaking engagements, syndicated newspaper columns, talk shows, professorships, and, if you're among the really, really fortunate, a seat on the Supreme Court of the United States of America!

You mean I can jump off the equal-opportunity treadmill and break through the glass ceiling to real *accomplishment?* Of course not. But you *can* distinguish yourself from the pack. You *can* disassociate yourself from gun-toting gang-bangers, drug-driven muggers, overbreeding dole-chiselers, civil rights poverty pimps, affirmative-action incompetents, L.A. rioters, Willie Horton, and all the usual suspects. You *can* have white people of substance treat you almost like you're somebody. (Of course, you still can't get a cab in Manhattan, but change doesn't happen overnight.)

This sounds like one of those pyramid schemes where the guy on top gets everything and the guy on the bottom gets gypped. Naturally it does. That's the American way. But this time [your name here] will be among the elite included in the highest echelons of upper-middle-class income, pseudopower, and quasi-prestige. And the best part? You'll never have to give another thought to those people you had to step over on the way up . . . unless you condescend to look down on them.

Still, what's the catch? The downside is that traditional knee-jerk, mealymouthed civil rights panderers will resent the fact that you've co-opted their historic monopoly on media access and brand you a traitor. Spike Lee may malign you on the silver screen. The few ghetto dwellers literate enough to catch you on a public affairs TV program will revile your name. Fortunately, Arsenio Hall and *In Living Color* are no longer around to make you the butt of their humor. To sum it up, there is no downside.

On the positive end, there'll be no more pretending to think equal-opportunity thoughts, when, in fact, your belief in quotas ended the minute you got your job because of one; no more acting as if you really believe a kente-cloth cummerbund is appropriate After 5 formal wear. Avant-garde intellectual publications will stop assigning you scholarly treatises on the postmodern theosophical and philological imagery underlying the thematic structure of Nikki Giovanni's poetry. You will never have to learn to dance like Janet Jackson. You can even continue to believe that Cleopatra looked just like Elizabeth Taylor, *and none of your peers will dispute you*!

Plus there's more. By joining the teeny (but highly visible) band of Black Conservative Spokespersons in America, you'll find yourself in the right place at the right time when it comes to media access. Virtually within moments of announcing your new job title, you'll be trading bons mots with Charlie Rose and Ted Koppel. Or trashing the welfare state along with ace boon-coon compadres like Safire, Will, Buchanan, Limbaugh, and Howard Stern. Or playing musical chairs with Oprah, Sally, Phil, Larry, and Geraldo. Even snubbing Bryant!

Sound too good to be true? One satisfied neo-Negro, Shelby Steele, used to be one of the many run-of-the-mill cogs in one of the many run-of-the-mill wheels that form California's university system—that is, until he wrote a book expressing attitudes that could have fallen from the lips of the Republican leadership in Congress. Quicker than you can say "entitlement," Steele became a multimedia event . . . *despite the fact that no one could be found who had actually read his book*! That's the kind of meteoric success you can expect by taking advantage of this tremendous career opportunity.

Plus you'll make friends and influence people while partying at some of the most discriminatory private clubs in America. The Heritage Foundation will go out of its way to listen to your opinion before it disregards it. Congressmen, heads of state, and Jesse Helms will have you by for brunch. Dan Quayle will think of you as an intellectual equal. You can opt between Billy Graham, Jerry Falwell, or Reverend Moon as your personal spiritual adviser. Not to mention that on Sunday morning, which you used to spend ripping out want ads, you'll be leisurely looking up your listing on the *New York Times* best-seller list. Unless, of course, McLaughlin needs you.

It's a life, and it's yours simply for making a slight attitude adjustment.

1. IS MY ATTITUDE POLITICALLY CORRECT?

Except in extreme cases (like if you're a direct descendant of Booker T. Washington, Uncle Tom, or Uncle Ben), it probably isn't. Most African-Americans were not raised to believe that the worst thing that could have happened to the civil rights movement was getting some of what they asked for.

This is why Black conservatives are usually *made* instead of born. However, the process of pulling yourself up by your bootstraps and becoming one of the lucky few is easier if you have a natural inclination toward the philosophical basis of conservatism. (It is also easier, but not an absolute prerequisite, if you have something to conserve.)

Should any of the items on the following list apply to you, you're already a step up the ladder to achieving that right-wingy edge. If not, perhaps you could use a little more politically incorrect, culturally literate indoctrination. Try taking a Latin as a Second Language course or memorizing the collected works of Ayn Rand while whistling the Mantovani version of "Yesterday."

Your attitude is politically correct if

You are embarrassed that you got your Ivy League acceptance through racial quotas, even though George Bush was never embarrassed that he got his Yale acceptance through the legacy quota that makes room for below-average descendants of above-average wealth.

You are embarrassed that you got your job through affirmative action, even though no one of your particular ethnic persuasion ever got your particular job through fair employment practices.

You worry that your white colleagues laugh at your qualifications behind your back despite the fact that you're overqualified.

You regret your close personal relationship with Huey P. Newton during the excessively turbulent and misguided sixties and sincerely understand that Barry Goldwater was a choice, not an echo.

You tried to resurrect Young Americans for Freedom at Morehouse College.

You are an editor at the *Dartmouth Review*.

You are a Whiffenpoof.

You fell in love with the law after the Bakke decision.

You fell in love with the law because of the Clarence Thomas hearings.

You fell in love with the law the moment Earl Warren stepped down.

You live in Simi Valley.

You're the only nonwhite member in your Episcopal congregation.

You're the only nonwhite resident in your neighborhood.

You're the only nonwhite resident in your home.

It is your opinion that LA Police Chief Daryl Gates was not tough enough on crime.

It is your opinion that we are not building enough prisons.

It is your opinion that Marion Barry should be executed for embarrassing the race and, while we're at it, we should nuke the boyz 'n the 'hood.

It is your opinion that the Rodney King jury showed extraordinary insight.

You feel the decline of Western civilization began with the advent of Afro-American studies.

You feel the decline of Western civilization began with the advent of women's studies.

You feel the decline of Western civilization began the day rapper Flava Flav became a clue in the *New York Times* daily crossword puzzle.

It is your opinion that welfare mothers, including the one who bore you, are just too lazy to work.

It is your opinion that welfare mothers, except for the one who bore you, would be better off with forced sterilization.

You tried to make Nancy Reagan an honorary Alpha Kappa Alpha.

You practice benign neglect.

You sound like William Buckley.

Since Ronald Reagan no longer has the capacity to remember how he devastated the Black community with his policies, neither will you.

2. WHERE DO I SIGN UP?

In order to achieve the position of Black Conservative Spokesperson, you must first bring large amounts of attention to yourself and your culturally unorthodox opinions. This is most easily done by writing a book or staging a media event, but there are other alternatives. Sexually harassing Anita Hill seems to be one surefire means of getting your name out there. Unfortunately, it's already been done.

There is also the possibility of committing an outrageous act connected to a notorious public figure who is guaranteed media coverage—like marrying Pat Buchanan's daughter, for instance, if only procreation had been included among his many talents. (You could also have a very public affair with Ron Reagan, Jr., but unless you're female, this could undermine your credibility.)

Some other suggestions for getting your name before the public:

Sponsor a comic tribute to Rush Limbaugh

How about Barbra Streisand as host and Paul Rodriguez as comic relief? Oops! We forgot . . . no FemiNazi Jews or *pachucos* allowed! Let's try it again. Bob Hope as roastmaster, Barry ("I am not a Jew") Goldwater as roastmaster emeritus, Phil Gramm as jokemeister, Peggy Noonan as writer/jokestress, and Mary Matalin as writer/dominatrix. Refreshments to be provided by politically amenable companies like Coors and Domino's Pizza. Up with People will entertain. Plus Tondelayo, the curvaceous octoroon star of *Do the Right Wing*, will be available in the men's room for uplifting conversation. The best conservative minds in the country will join in this laughfest. (Unfortunately, Negroes aren't welcome, but everyone will appreciate your effort.)

Volunteer as a speechwriter for Strom Thurmond

People like yourself are sophisticated enough to understand that being pro-white is not the same as being a racist, so put your beliefs to work. Be assured that in no time the *New York Times*, the *Washington Post*, and several lusty Ku Klux Klanettes will be vying for your unlisted number.

Write a fan letter to Jesse Helms

Something simple, sweet—for example: I'm Black and I like the way you eliminated race as an issue in your last election campaign.

Attend Yale Law School

Inevitably, you'll be asked to testify for or against some of your fellow colleagues. For example, Yale Law professor Stephen L. Carter was on the *Today* show as a character witness for both Clarence Thomas *and* Anita Hill, which also gave him a wonderful opportunity to plug his anti–affirmative action book.

Move next door to Newt Gingrich

Once Newtie gets past the decline in property values, he may ask your advice on where to find loyal Negro servants.

Create a religion

White men in power sometimes have difficulty acknowledging a Black person in a leadership position who is not wearing a clerical collar. This is because the only time they ever recognized a Black person in a leadership position was during the civil rights movement, when they could limit him to leading his own people to Bull Conner's dogs. Be that as it may, you can take advantage of this by assembling the First Reform Church of the Latter Day Booker T's, where the emphasis is on self-help, no government handouts, and elimination of miscegenation.

Hey, it worked for Elijah Muhammad!

Write a book questioning affirmative action and quotas

Okay, it's been done before, but it's the kind of message America never gets tired of hearing.

3. DOES THIS MAKE ME A NEO–AFRO CON?

We live in a country with labels, and no matter how much you try to get around it, everyone wants to be able to easily pigeonhole you by slapping on some code name. Fortunately, this is America, and in matters other than abortion, you have a choice!

Just think of it this way: Booker T. Washington was **Colored.** A. Philip Randolph was a **Negro.** Stokely Carmichael was **Black.** Thurgood Marshall was the world's last remaining **Afro-American.** Jesse Jackson is an **African-American.** You can be any of the above just by deciding for yourself which one of these names, if any, is appropriate for someone of your political beliefs. To help your decision along, try this little quiz:

1. I am not an **Afro-American** because:
   a. I have never heard of a country called Afro.
   b. My ancestors did not emigrate from a country called Afro.
   c. My hair is not nappy enough for an Afro.

2. I am not an **African-American** because:
   a. I have never been to Africa.
   b. I have never seen *Roots*.
   c. No one in my family speaks Swahili.

3. I am not **Black** because:
   a. I am actually a nice taffy color.
   b. I am actually a delicious chocolate color.
   c. I come from a family of Negroes.

4. I am not a **Negro** because:
   a. Sixties militants used that word pejoratively to describe handkerchief-headed, Uncle Tommin', retrograde bootlickers—none of which refers to myself.
   b. I was never comfortable with the way southerners pronounced the word.
   c. *Negro* translates to "black" in Spanish. I have no Hispanic ancestry, nor do I resemble a tar baby.

5. I am not **Colored** because:
   a. I refuse to pay dues to a radical leftist organization like the NAACP.
   b. It's too much of a reminder of those signs on Dixie rest rooms.
   c. The term always made me feel like an Easter egg.

6. I am not **Creole** because:
   a. None of my many white forefathers are from New Orleans.
   b. I do not like gumbo.
   c. No one would believe it.

7. I am not **biracial** because:
   a. I am not sure if that word refers to those of us with Native American ancestry.
   b. I am not sure if that word refers to those of us with white slaveholding ancestors.
   c. I am not sure who my father is.

8. I am not an **assimilationist** because:
   a. I got rhythm.
   b. I can play basketball.
   c. I taught my white wife how to cook ham hocks.

CULTURALLY LITERATE GLOSSARY

African-Americans Persons whose antecedents worked as unremunerated laborers in the slave trade.

AIDS The only means God could find to get rid of Roy Cohn.

American Indians People who tried to get in the way of the *real* Native Americans: the red-blooded (not red-skinned) pioneers who fought their way across the plains in covered wagons and paved paradise to put up a parking lot.

antiwar movement Means by which those of

superior status were able to move into the National Guard and avoid service in Vietnam.

Murphy Brown   Emmy-winning leftist slut who should have had an abortion if anyone should have, which they shouldn't.

civil rights movement   Martin Luther King, Jr., marched in Montgomery to help a Black woman whose feet hurt, thereby causing a racial rift that has yet to be settled forty years later.

Christopher Columbus   *Discoverer* of America, a land inhabited by naked, ignorant savages who were dumb enough to sell Manhattan for a handful of cubic zirconium. It is fortunate for these aboriginals that Columbus *discovered* them before the Japanese did.

cultural elite   Those people who know who they are.

Bob Dole   Man who has proven that a physical disability does not have to limit its bearer to compassion, empathy, or understanding.

entitlements (Social Security)   If you're a person over sixty-five who can still manage to drag yourself to the voting booth, you're entitled to everything you can get.

entitlements (welfare) If you're an amoral whore who's multiplying like maggots with illegitimate babies, you're entitled to receive a financial incentive to have more babies.

family values One dad. One mom. Two kids. No sex.

GOP God-fearing Ovarian Police.

Anita Hill Lying bitch.

Japan Sneaky, post-Togo isolationist country that maintains a superior attitude because it did not invent the Edsel or the Pinto. Frequently forgets that lazy, incompetent American workers created the Enola Gay.

Michael Jordan Arrogant, belligerent former basketball tosser and lousy minor leaguer whose unpatriotic stance in turning down a White House photo-op request makes us especially sorry Larry Bird retired.

Jack Kemp Rubbed jockstraps with more Black males than any other conservative.

Martin Luther King, Jr. Rabble-rousing, whoremongering Communist plagiarist who flouted the law and gave J. Edgar Hoover many titillating moments.

Leave it to Beaver   Reality-based fifties sitcom depicting a typical all-American nuclear family where father knows best, mom knows kitchens, kids know nonviolent high jinks, maids know their place, and Bo knows the location of the back of the bus. A virtual plethora of average American experiences. See also *Beulah*.

Malcolm X   Better dead than read.

Thurgood Marshall   Cranky old bastard who consistently remained on the wrong side of the law.

Mickey Mouse   Contrary to appearances, an Aryan.

National Endowment for the Arts   A crypto–porn factory propagating homosexual activity among Black males with abnormally enormous penises. Also condones urinating on Christ for the fun of it. Provided primary influence for Charles Manson.

Operation Rescue   God's chosen wombwardens.

Richard Nixon   Statesman, diplomat, and, despite appearances, never really Diane Sawyer's main squeeze.

Pablo Picasso   Brilliant modern artist who taught Africans how to design masks.

Plato, Aristotle et al.   Philosophers who form the basis of Western thought. It is interesting that in the nearly two and a half millennia since their deaths, not one minority or female has come up with anything better.

Soon-Yi Previn   Rosemary's baby.

pro-abortionists   Radical, often husbandless and homely feminists who want to screw around with any Tom, Harry, or Dick and then use abortion to kill the baby when it interferes with their lifestyle. Anti-family, anti-American, anti-God, and antithetical to the world as we know it.

Ronald Reagan   The greatest President this nation has ever known. Better when senile than most men with all their faculties.

right-to-life movement   Believers in the sanctity of life of unborn fetuses (who better be able to take care of themselves once we get them through the birth canal).

school prayer   Practice that separates Newt Gingrich from Satan worshipers. (And while we're at it, let's put the Christ back in Xmas.)

supply-side economics   Theory that allows the rich to get richer and the poor to suck up the remains from the crumb-sweeper.

Clarence Thomas   Man who rose from abject, degrading, personality-warping poverty to survive a high-tech lynching and occupy one of the most exalted positions in the land. Our nig.

welfare dependency   The content of their character.

welfare reform   By forcing people off their backs and into jobs that cannot begin to provide them with enough money for food, shelter, health care, or the Cadillac they all drive, we are not only endowing them with fewer hours in the day to get pregnant, we are also creating substantial business opportunities for investors in the prison and orphanage industries.

Talxploitation

Television

*I*f all the best African-American minds in the country were put together in one room, what would be the first subject to come up for discussion?

1. economics
2. the Republican Congress
3. teen violence and/or pregnancy
4. welfare reform
5. multicultural education

or

6. Who are those finger-wagging/head-bob-bing/eye-bucking/neck-swiveling Black people who show up on daytime television talk shows and where do they come from?

I think we can safely go with number 6, which leads to some additional questions:

If a tree falls in the forest and Montel isn't there to stick a microphone in its face, does it still make a noise?

Do Geraldo and Rolonda have a licensed finger-wagging/head-bobbing/eye-bucking/neck-swiveling practitioner warm up their audiences?

Which came first, the camera or the attitude?

Just wondering.

Not that there is anything wrong with finger wagging/head bobbing/eye bucking/neck swivel-ing, as long as these are done tastefully. It's just that many of us find it curious why these activities have spread like a plague among African-American participants in certain types of TV formats. Could there be a recessive gene that mutates and makes you want to holler when the camera goes on? Does the heat from the studio lights dynamically interact with melanin, producing a throwback to ancient nonverbal communication rituals? Does Jerry Springer pass out twenties to the most inspirational finger-wagging/head-bobbing/eye-bucking neck swiveler? Again, I wonder.

It's understandable that daytime talk-show participants starved for attention would do anything, and say anything, to get it, particularly from a national audience. It's unconscionable, and probably immoral, that tacky television talk-show hosts starved for audience ratings will exploit anyone to get them. Let's be real here; the impact of these images is not benign. As a people, we may have survived Little Black Sambo, Old Black Joe, Stepin Fetchit, Tarzan, Prissy, Mammy, Buckwheat, Uncle Ben, Uncle Tom, Uncle Remus, and Al Jolson in blackface, but I'm not sure we'll make it past *Jenny Jones*.

For this reason, my personal organization, the NAAACE (Non–finger-wagging/head-bobbing/eye-bucking/neck-swiveling African-Americans Against Callous Exploitation), has decided it is time for the medium presenting these stereotypes to make a sincere effort to offset their impact.

How would this be possible? By changing the stereotypes into crime-fighting superheroes, of course.

To this end, we are offering, free of charge, an outline for a television series that turns negative talk-show images into positive role models for children of all races, colors, and creeds.

To: Fox Television Network
Re: Series Pilot

"ATTACK OF THE TEENAGE MUTANT TALK SHOW GUESTS"

CONCEPT

In a unique format reminiscent of *Baywatch* with a ghetto attitude, *The A-Team* with all the roles played by Mr. T, or an action-packed, home-boyesque *Cosby Show* (without the mother and father characters), *Attack of the Teenage Mutant Talk Show Guests* is the first action/adventure television series to synthesize the fascinating team effort required in gang-banging with the exciting, provocative drama inherent in Black teenagers' appearances on afternoon talk shows. Underscored by the raw violence and energy of gangsta rap, each weekly one-hour episode will feature four teenagers who go undercover as guests on *Ricki Lake* by day and solve exciting crimes when not on the air.

They are assisted in their activities by their kindly truant officer, Mr. Kotter, a nuclear physicist who lost his government clearance during the McCarthy era, and D'André, a former hardcore drug dealer recently returned from prison who is now in the process of founding his own religion and inner-city day-care center. Also featured on a semiregular basis will be Taekwanda, a martial arts instructor who doubles as a manicurist, hairstylist, and finger-wagging/head-bobbing/eye-bucking/neck-swiveling coach for the gang's talk-show appearances.

CASTING PROFILE

> RICKI LAKE: *Shrewd, ambitious, white female talk-show host, age 22 to 27*

During each episode, the greatest skill required of Ms. Lake (or the actress playing her role) is pretending not to be aware that all the guests on her talk show are actually the same four people in different disguises.

> QUANTEESHA: *African-American female, age 15 to 19, weight over 180*

Quanteesha, who can talk and chew gum at the same time, is recognized coast-to-coast for her ability to pronounce *girlfriend* in five syllables. With a "mixed-media" hairdo (sprayed-gold marcel waves glued to one side, a retro–Farrah Fawcett on the other, and Shirley Temple curls pinned to the back) and a penchant for size-eighteen Daisy Dukes shorts, Quanteesha is frequently at a disadvantage during undercover operations. Her secret weapon when under attack involves whipping off her leggings and, with one quick spandex snap, rendering her adversary speechless.

SUPER G-MAN (aka Calvin): *African-American male, age 16 to 18, buff body (as if he'd spent time incarcerated), sexually attractive to white females ages 13 to 49*

As an undercover talk-show guest, Super G-Man specializes in topics such as, "Yeah, I slept with my woman's best friend," "Yeah, I slept with my woman's sister," "Yeah, I slept with my woman's mother," and "The bitch asked for it." Self-described as "a Taurus with a penis rising," his gangsta exterior is merely a cover-up for a gangsta interior. A fast talker, though not necessarily comprehensible, Super G-Man is particularly sensitive to people who dis him or step on his authentic suede Ralph Lauren Polo hiking boots. His secret weapon is a 9-mm automatic displayed at all times.

HAMPTON: *African-American male geek, age 18 to 20, pitiful body*

With his mild-mannered, homely wimp front, Hampton is the talk-show guest who appears as if he could never attract a woman. Yet he always has at least two. Both pregnant. Expecting twins. With the same due date. Hampton's secret weapon is that underneath the Steve Urkel facade lies a man who could win a Long Dong Silver "look-alike" contest. When in danger, Hampton reaches into his wallet, pulls out an extrajumbo, made-to-measure, bespoke condom and wields it as a bullwhip.

CREEM: *African-American female, age 19, built like a brick . . . umm . . . house*

As an undercover talk-show guest, Creem specializes in playing the other woman. With her vast wig collection, featuring a neo–Loni Anderson motif, and her personally designed collection of faux Frederick's of Hollywood After 5 'hoodwear, she can change her appearance more often than Madonna changes sexual preferences. Creem's crime-fighting ability lies in her perfectly manicured five-inch fingernails imbedded with letters spelling out her code name: H-O-T-

T-T-S-T-U-F-F. Each press-and-stick nail is made of cubic zirconium, which, when poked in an enemy's chest area, leaves an imperceptible pattern of little tiny holes, causing the victim slowly and unknowingly to leak precious bodily fluids.

"ATTACK OF THE TEENAGE MUTANT TALK SHOW GUESTS" PILOT SCRIPT SYNOPSIS

FADE IN on a break in the taping of a *Ricki Lake* episode entitled "My Man Moved His Woman into Our Bedroom and Now She's Hogging the Covers." CREEM's beeper goes off. Although it's almost time for the fight scene where she rips QUANTEESHA's wig off and tosses it to Grrrraldo, SUPER G-MAN's pit bull, CREEM hurriedly dials Action Central and finds the team has been assigned a case. It seems Marky Mark has fallen off the rap charts and they must find a way to get him back.

After the show, the team rushes to the offices of Calvin Klein, who once had Marky Mark in his boxers. They learn Mr. Klein now refers to Mark as an "ersatz thug" and has switched his advertising campaign to the real thing: Mike Tyson lying in his Skivvies on a bearskin rug, saying, "Nothing comes between me and my Calvins."

The TEENAGE MUTANT TALK SHOW GUESTS split up. HAMPTON checks out a Video Soul taping at the local affiliate of Black Entertainment Television and finds, to his consternation, that Marky Mark isn't Black. SUPER G-MAN drops in at Trump Towers, where he shares an aperitif with the Donald and leaves a deposit on a sumptuous half-room luxury apartment home with a tasteful marble waterfall in the dining alcove.

QUANTEESHA and CREEM head for the *National Enquirer* offices. Displaying quivering cleavage to divert the security guard, CREEM allows QUANTEESHA to sneak up behind and apply her patented double-reverse thigh squish (which is under consideration for Olympic competition). They read a past issue of the paper and locate their quarry.

CUT TO a Connecticut hideaway where Marky Mark is taking secret soul-singing lessons from Michael Bolton. With an earsplitting rallying cry of "Feets don't fail me now," THE TEENAGE MUTANT TALK SHOW GUESTS fly into the room through an open window. Along with Mark and Bolton, they record a 1995 rap update of James Brown's "Say It Loud (I'm Black and I'm Proud)," which will be released as a single at a later date. Then THE TEENAGE MUTANT TALK SHOW GUESTS go off alone to rehearse the next day's

Ricki Lake topic: "My Man's Mother Always Picks on Me Just Because I'm Dark-Skinned and Live in Her House and Don't Pay Rent and Don't Clean up Because I'm Not Her Maid."
FADE OUT.

Take Me

to My

Leader

*T*here are some things about leadership that thoroughly confuse me. I understand that Bill Clinton is America's head honcho—whether some voters like it or not—because people *elected* him. Rudolph Giuliani is mayor of all New Yorkers—whether I like it or not—because some of them *elected* him. Jean-Bertrand Aristide was the *elected* leader of Haiti, even when the CIA wouldn't let him be.

Randal Terry of Operation Rescue has been chosen to speak for fetally obsessed wombwardens who don't understand why God made sex a requirement of procreation and hope to be reincarnated as the Virgin Mary's spiritual adviser. People for the Ethical Treatment of Animals play point man for leather shoe–wearing animal-rights activists who feel free to discriminate against cows. The Reverend Donald Wildmon of the American Family Institute is the anointed voice of those who are forced to feed their kids fried-grits-on-pork-rind sandwiches seven nights a week because they hocked their food stamps trying to get a few dollars together to contribute to wiping out the National Endowment for the Arts.

Yes, there's more.

When the head of the American Jewish Congress makes a statement, it's on behalf of the people who appointed him as head of the American Jewish Congress. When Cesar Chavez cried

"Huerta!" he was representing the people who had elected him president of the United Farm Workers and those who identified with his battle.

The point is (finally): So why don't African-Americans get to elect their own leaders?

I don't mean to imply that anybody with a placard and an attitude who manages to worm his way onto the six o'clock news is referred to as my leader by the media. Sometimes it just seems that way. However, it should be noted that most of the people I know wouldn't follow Colin Powell anywhere, including Kuwait. (Yes, I know he doesn't have an attitude or a placard. That's part of his problem.)

COMMON MYTH ABOUT BLACK LEADERS #1:

One size fits all.

In order for there to be one (1) singular Black leader to appeal to all African-Americans, he or she would have to have to be a three-piece-suited, Wall Street–based, Howard to Harvard–educated, blue-collar, gangsta-rappin', slamdunkin', homey/ 'ho conservative entrepreneur with a name preceded by a religious title. This does not seem to describe Louis Farrakhan, so we can scratch him from the list.

COMMON MYTH ABOUT
BLACK LEADERS #2:

Black people need to be led.

Most of the African-Americans of my acquaintance manage to get to work, pay their rent, raise their kids, and occasionally have a good time without Jesse Jackson giving them directions. Jesse is busy paying his own rent. I'm sure he'd be glad to speak out on the big picture when necessary; occasionally, he might even run for President or something. I might even vote for him. But he'd still be a *presidential candidate*, not a shepherd with a flock.

COMMON MYTH ABOUT
BLACK LEADERS #3:

African-Americans will vote for any **candidate who is Black.**

Here are some of the things I was sure I'd never do in my life:

1. commit murder
2. sit through a 2 Live Crew concert
3. vote for Al Sharpton

So much for plans.

I couldn't help myself. He was running against Senator Daniel Moynihan, who once suggested that I and my ilk be dismissed with benign neglect, and who lately mentioned that unmarried mothers like myself were subverting the human species.

Actually, I would have loved to see Reverend Al going at it in the Senate with Jesse Helms. In a back-to-back filibuster. Mouth-to-mouth. Over civil rights legislation. As Muhammad Ali might say, "the thunda in the rotunda."

I swear I will never vote for Marion Barry.

COMMON MYTH ABOUT BLACK LEADERS #4:

Every Black leader is responsible for everything every other African-American says—ever.

Maybe it's just me, but if *New York Times* columnist Abe Rosenthal whines one more time about prominent Blacks not "denouncing" other African-Americans' questionable statements, I'm going to slap him. Not hard, because he might be litigious, but I am going to slap him.

Like, for instance: While talking about mass murderer Colin Ferguson, who went berserk on a commuter train because—oh who knows why?—former Farrakhan aide Khalid Abdul

Muhammad is quoted as saying, "God sent hurricanes, God sent earthquakes and, Goddammit, God sent Colin Ferguson."

Excuse me. I think it is obvious this man has a unique approach to this issue and very few others would consider it in the same way. To ask someone to "denounce" Muhammad's opinion implies that if they don't, or won't, they must agree. I don't think so. Here's a better idea. Let's get the "denounce" patrol to react to every public statement made by every prominent white man since the first Reagan inauguration. Retroactively. Take your time.

COMMON MYTH ABOUT
BLACK LEADERS #5:

They're all leading in the same direction.

Black revolution? Been there; done that. Corporate ladder climbing? Been there; done that. Antiwhite separatism? Ditto, and so on. The problem is some of us are moving left, some of us are moving right, and some of us who don't understand history are doomed to repeat it.

Maybe we should just start a weekly column in *Jet* magazine where potential leaders can, for a slight fee, enter their names along with the direction they plan to lead. Then people who would be happy to follow can leave their names on a voice-mail system. For example:

> Thomas, C.: Neocon/pro-porno/anti-
>   progress
> Doggy Dogg, S.: Pro-'hood/anti-
>   cop/gangsta capitalist
> Wattleton, F.: Pro-woman/pro-choice/
>   pro-family

That way, when an African-American claims to be speaking for Black people, it can be proved somebody's really listening.

Playing
the Race
Card

*M*aybe I'm just overly sensitive, but did anyone else besides me notice that African-Americans did not get mentioned in the Republican's 1994 contract with America? At least not specifically. Not unless we are supposed to take "welfare reform," "teenage pregnancy," and "more prisons" personally. Since I am not on welfare, my teenager is not pregnant, I have not RSVP'd for any upcoming incarceration commitments, and ditto for my immediate family members, it took a minute to realize we were the ones they were referring to. How silly of me.

From now on, I'll pay closer attention to code words. Particularly:

Us	Them
violence	farm subsidies
big city	savings-and-loan bailouts
moral degeneracy	mineral rights
food stamps	cattle grazing on public land
public housing	tax incentives for development
entitlements of the welfare variety	capital gains

In any case, America apparently held a referendum on African-Americans without bothering to call us by name. Pretty rude, if you ask me. I realize our forefathers were the strange fruit hanging from the American family tree, but 130 years after the end of slavery, you'd think people would be tired of treating our particular branch as if we're solely responsible for the root rot.

This is what concerns me: If you made a list of existence-challenged species, at this moment in time African-Americans would lie somewhere between the spotted owl and the dodo. And unfortunately, we aren't qualified for coverage under the Environmental Protection Act. Before I wake up one day to find my picture plastered on a milk carton, I think we should talk about this.

Oh, damn it, I forgot. We can't. Someone might accuse me of "playing the race card." I am not exactly sure what this means, but the press seems to whip it out whenever African-Americans raise the specter of racial bias—sort of like the way conservatives use "politically correct" to squelch dissenting thoughts; sort of like censorship by default.

Personally, I never really thought of racism as a game, so I haven't figured out how to play the race card. Maybe you start with a "race" deck of cards, which I'm sure can be obtained for a nominal (tax-deductible) contribution to either the Republican National Committee or the National Rifle Association. It's probably distinguished from regular playing decks by face cards with one-eyed Newts; Jesse, king of spades; and Hilary, red queen. More than likely, the four aces are decorated with wanted posters depicting Willie Horton, Marion Barry, Louis Farrakhan, and O. J. Simpson. There aren't any rules.

Of course, there is an off-chance that the press has a point with this "race card" business. Perhaps we African-Americans have just been too damn concerned about racial issues. Maybe we ought to take a cue from Howard Stern's jolly Black sidekick, Robin Quivers, and learn to laugh at ourselves. After all, what is the most important thing the sixties Black revolution had in common with the women's movement? No sense of humor. It's a joke. Lighten up.

You have to admit, we are hypersensitive on the subject of racism. Just because the cop who invaded O. J.'s house without a search warrant has mentioned in an official document that he hates African-Americans, we question his integrity. Just because the 1995 Republican-controlled Congress is trying to undermine funding for all social programs directed toward constituencies that did not vote for them, we take it as a personal attack. Like Newt and his Newtzis had time to consider the needs of every little teensy special-interest group.

Just think of our overreaction to things over the years. *Gone With the Wind*? An American classic sending a positive message about Negro loyalty that we're just too uptight to enjoy. *Amos 'n' Andy*? Wasn't forcing it off the air overkill? If we didn't think it was funny, we could have pushed the remote switch, if only it had been invented. It's a joke. Lighten up.

We must learn to admit that it's simply not possible for racism to lurk around every single, solitary, minute little corner. Think of it this way: No matter what we *sense*, racial antipathy is not necessarily hiding under New York mayor Rudy Giuliani's hairpiece. Political expediency is possibly hiding under Rudy Giuliani's hairpiece, but not necessarily racism. Perhaps Rush Limbaugh tells jokes in illiterate Black dialect simply because he appreciates our entertainment value. Who knows. In fact, who really knows what evil lurks in the hearts of men? Only the Shadow, and he didn't do so well at the box office last year.

If I were white (it's a joke . . . lighten up), I'm sure I'd be sick of hearing about racism by now. For four hundred years, African-Americans and their liberal backers have refused to let sleeping dogs lie. Those danged abolitionists talked it to death. The civil rights people threw it in everyone's face for years.

Didn't we go through that affirmative-action/equal-opportunity business just so we could end this conversation? Okay, so it didn't work, but whose fault is that? The beleaguered white male, dare we ask? In the immortal words of Milli Vanilli, let's just "blame it on the rain" and be done with it. Consider the situation *handled* and move on to a postracist society. The loose ends will get wrapped up when we get around to it. It's time racism was over. It's time not to talk about it anymore.

Of course it's hard to change habits. When you've spent your life calling taxi drivers racist for passing you by for a white fare, when you're raised on calling corporations racist when they won't hire any African-American executives, when you call Strom Thurmond a racist because . . . well . . . that's what he is, it's hard to put up a peace sign and let bygones be bygones.

But maybe there is another way to look at reality. Maybe we've been seeing things that aren't really there. Hey, paranoia happens. Some people see UFO's everywhere; some people see racism. Some people hear voices; some people hear racial slurs. Could be that they're all part of the same phenomena. What we need is a new way of looking at racial issues. With a little analysis, we might find alternative explanations for everyday occurrences that might have seemed to have a negative connotation.

For instance: Based on an unsubstantiated, unscientific study, it appears that not one audience member of any David Letterman late-night show since the beginning of time has been Black.

This does not necessarily mean African-Americans are excluded from entering. Maybe Letterman provides special, extra-rosy lighting that blends all audience members, regardless of race, color, creed, or country of origin, into one pleasing skin tone. Maybe writing for tickets in advance is antithetical to African-American cultural origins. Maybe we're waiting for Arsenio to come back. Whatever, you can't blame everything on racism.

Another for instance: The NAACP became null and void after opening communications with Louis Farrakhan, which is disarmingly similar to what happened to Andy Young when, as a UN envoy, he opened communications with the Palestinians. This is not necessarily déjà vu all over again. There could be some logical explanation for this startlingly odd coincidence. Shit happens.

I understand that changing our preprogrammed mind-set will not be easy; lifelong patterns are difficult to reverse. But if we are going to stop relying on playing the race card, African-Americans are going to have to look at life from another perspective. With this in mind, here are some alternative explanations for situations that, in other, happier times, we would have ascribed to just plain racism.

Possible alternative explanations to what we traditionally perceived as racism:

The suggestion of orphanages for children of unwed teenage mothers

1. Orphanages eliminate welfare payments.
2. They provide companionship for only children.
3. They free the mother from having to hire a baby-sitter for prom night.

The nomination of Clarence Thomas to the Supreme Court

1. He really was the most qualified Black man in America.
2. Barbara Bush thought he was a hunk.
3. Justice Thomas is actually the last remaining member of the Symbionese Liberation Army, and, when we least expect it, he will kidnap Patti Davis and force her to rob banks.

The fact that it appears no African-American has ever won Ed McMahon's American Family Sweepstakes

1. Mr. McMahon prefers to provide African-Americans with opportunities to win on *Star Search*.
2. When Mr. McMahon named his sweepstakes American Family, he forgot to notify his staff that African-American families were part of that category.
3. A glitch in Mr. McMahon's computer pro-

gram eliminates inner-city addresses from his mailing list.

The Rodney King beating

1. Mr. King could have been hiding a weapon in his shoe.
2. Mr. King could have been hiding a weapon in his teeth.
3. Mr. King could have been a rogue member of the A-Team and/or the Incredible Hulk's first cousin, with superhuman cop-killing abilities.

Cutting off funds for the Congressional Black Caucus

1. The money saved is going to provide more government cheese.
2. The money saved is going to provide additional employment opportunities in congressional hallways for African-American bootblacks.
3. The money saved is going to pay for .003 percent of tomorrow's interest on the national deficit.

Building prisons instead of funding youth programs

1. Prisons provide nifty employment opportunities for otherwise unskilled and unemployable African-American guards.

2. If your child is safe in prison, you don't have to worry about him getting hurt in the streets.
3. Prisons relieve overcrowding in schools.

Disproportionate locating of toxic-waste dumps in minority neighborhoods

1. Toxic-waste dumps provide a quick and easy way to create compost.
2. Toxic-waste dump residents never have to fear losing their homes through gentrification.
3. Eventually, toxic-waste dumps relieve overcrowding in schools.

The scuttling of Lani Guinier's Justice Department nomination

1. Ms. Guinier didn't understand that "one man, one vote" cannot be used to persecute whites who will soon attain minority status in this country.
2. Ms. Guinier underestimated the alliterative impact of "quota queen."
3. Ms. Guinier was not discriminating enough about guests at her wedding.

The election of white Republican Rudy Giuliani over African-American Democrat David Dinkins in traditionally Democratic New York City

1. After one term, it was time for a change.
2. Rigid, uptight voters, sympathetic to Giuliani's rigid, uptight personality, turned out in droves.
3. Balding voters, sympathetic to Giuliani's tacky hairpiece, turned out in droves.

The return of states' rights

1. Orval Faubus is dead and George Wallace might as well be, so it can't be a return of the fifties.
2. Blacks can vote everywhere, even though they don't, so it can't be a return of the pre–civil rights era.
3. The states are more likely than the federal government to distribute services equally and fairly, regardless of race, color, creed, country of origin, or who has the most power, earns the biggest income, and pays the most taxes, so it can't be a return of Reconstruction.

Welfare reform

1. The country is willing to provide equal and adequate education, along with employment opportunities, so everyone can become self-supporting.
2. The country is willing to have open and free discussions of birth control, abortions, and family planning so that teenagers can

learn to prevent pregnancy without feeling guilty.

3. The country is willing to provide teenagers with options and possibilities, so they don't have to look at childbearing as their only "positive" achievement in life.

(This last one is obviously a joke. Lighten up.)

The Organic Free-Range African-American Child

A Twelve-Step Program for Creating Unincarcerated, Unpregnant, Undead African-American Children

1. Do not let them listen to anything but gangsta rap.

Kurt Cobain committed suicide, Sid Vicious murdered his girlfriend, Bob Dylan became a Jew for Jesus, John Lennon and Elvis were drug addicts, and Leonard Bernstein hid his baton in the closet. Obviously, there is nothing positive to learn from any form of white music.

2. Do not teach them about sex.

What they don't know can't hurt them, particularly since chastity belts are not available at K Mart and saltpeter is not covered by Medicaid.

3. Do not teach them to read.

This way, they will avoid all the negative stereotypes that appear in the print media and will learn their own history orally, just like the griot who remembered Alex Haley's ancestors in *Roots*. (This will also put them in sync with Leonard Jeffries, the CCNY African-American studies professor who is too much of a scholar to publish.)

4. Do not let them talk to white people.

History has proven that integration leads to low self-esteem.

5. Do not make them go to school.

Unfortunately, there is no other way to sidestep armed debates between Uzi-toting fellow matriculants. Besides, according to one white man who made many millions of dollars by passing on this information, everything you need to know, you learn in kindergarten.

6. Do not let them leave the 'hood.

They will only get confused when "others" do not recognize the value of their $125 sneakers, their gold jewelry, and their ability to write a rap song while simultaneously flipping a dozen Big Macs.

7. Never allow them to ask a police officer for assistance.

How do you tell a "good" cop from a rabid one? They all look alike! Fortunately, officers who enter your neighborhood are so busy shaking down drug dealers, it is not likely that your child will encounter one except when being asked to assume the position.

8. Do not let them eat at Denny's.

Denny's claims to have solved its little institutionalized racism problem, but a Pullman porter once told me that when he didn't like the attitude of the white people he was serving, he'd spit in their food. A word to the wise is sufficient.

9. Only allow them to watch films starring Wesley Snipes, Tupac Shakur, or Arnold Schwarzenegger.

According to the noted Black filmmaker Fred Williamson, the racist white media dogs/executives who run Hollywood will not allow positive, loving films to be made about African-Americans. Since we can't have sex, we'll make do with violence.

10. Do not allow your daughters anywhere in the vicinity of white males.

"White men can't jump" is a historically proven fallacy when applied to Black women.

11. Do not expose them to the Protestant work ethic.

Why teach work ethics when there are no longer any ethics in the workplace? Not to mention that considering the jobless rate for African-Americans, your child is as likely to get a leading role in a Woody Allen movie as he/she is to find employment that offers more than minimum wage and a lifetime supply of two all-beef-patties-special-sauce-lettuce-cheese-pickles-onions-on-a-sesame-seed-bun.

12. Do not send them to church.

Martin Luther King, Jr., turned the other cheek, and you see where it got him.

Let's Get

Busy

A Grouchy Elegy

*I*t is not true that since he went off the air last year, Arsenio Hall has been:

1. singing backup for Luther Vandross
2. working as the fifth Top
3. managing the Pips
4. acting as a stand-in for Jean-Claude Van Damme
5. still interviewing Louis Farrakhan

Arsenio Hall? So why are you bringing him up?

Like they used to say on *Family Feud*, good question.

Since he's been off the air, every night at 11:30 my TV set seems a little lonelier. A little less lively. A little less multicultural. A little more Eurocentric. Okay, a lot more white. It's as if I used to get a formal invitation to watch every night and now I'm just any old party crasher who can't count on being in sync with the host, the music, the guests, the establishment, or the vibes.

Not that I can argue with the complaint that Arsenio sometimes had the interviewing skills of Mr. Rogers. There was that weird little habit of saying "hmmmmmmmm" to an answer when he was busy anticipating the next question. There was that inability to go for the natural follow-up question because it wasn't written on a card. There was that tendency to get silly and personal, which could leave the audience feeling like the show was going on without them.

And yes, I'll admit it, I didn't always choose to watch *The Arsenio Hall Show* every night, probably because I am just too damned old for hip-hop before bedtime. I couldn't take Salt-n-Pepa on a full stomach. I didn't want to see raging homophobes like Chuck D of Public Enemy talk about being positive. I didn't want to hear Tupac Shakur's philosophy of women. And until he understands that women are his equal, not people to be revered, not people to be respected, but his equal, I don't want to hear Louis Farrakhan say anything. But that's just a personal reaction.

Arsenio gave media access to a segment of America that never sees itself included in the mainstream: rap artists, down-on-their-luck R & B artists, gang-bangers, butch comedians, disabled comedians with speech impediments, over-the-hill athletes. How many times did you ever see Sistah Souljah hanging out on the couch next to Johnny Carson? Could David Letterman have calmed down the L.A. uprising? Would Jay Leno have used his stage to solidify a gang truce? (Yeah, right. Only if he was televising from a tank with storm troopers as backup.)

Entertainment with a social agenda: Sometimes it worked, and sometimes it didn't, but it required you to have an opinion. One major white TV critic said he "just didn't get it"; African-American audiences don't get *Seinfeld*, but that doesn't stop anyone from putting it on the air. Dozens of other white critics hinted that Arsenio's show was just "too Black." Hmmmmmmmmm . . . guess what I thought of *Thirtysomething*? There was nothing about the characters that could make me want to leap the cultural divide in order to get to know their whiny little asses better. I, however, wasn't being paid to be an "objective" critic.

The twenty-plus cutting-edgers of my acquaintance dropped Arsenio about thirty seconds after he came on the air because, they claimed, he had this lousy habit of sucking up to white people. Mo' better, he should have limited his interviews to five hours a week of Spike Lee, perhaps? Nobody ever got rich by trying to make all Black people happy at the same time. Well, maybe Arsenio did, but he paid for it.

The claim was he went off the air because his audience deserted him. More to the point, broadcast politics did him in. Many of his affiliates were sold to the Fox network, which had its own late-night plans, leaving him homeless in much of the country. Media attention centered on the Jay/Dave/Chevy(?!) Battle of the Network Night Guys, as if Arsenio wasn't even part of the competition. Critics who had dismissed him from the outset no longer even pretended he existed. Just like they still pretend his audience doesn't exist. Just like the networks pretend his audience doesn't exist so they don't have to program for it.

Of course, since African-Americans didn't scream loudly when *The Arsenio Hall Show* was in trouble, the networks know they can continue to act as if we don't exist. It's the American way.

As for Arsenio, if he gets bored with retirement, maybe he can get back into the business of producing late-night, race-appropriate programming. Otherwise, put money on some syndicator trying to reach Black viewers with:

> *Psychic Star Search*, hosted by Ed McMahon
>   and LaToya Jackson
> *Slick Rick's Rap-O-Mania*, coming live from
>   Mr. Rick's prison cell
> *The Flava Flav Comedy Hour*
> *Def Jam Religious Gems*
>   or possibly
> *The Iceberg Slim Literary Hour*

It's time.

Sheniqua

Had a Baby

(Can't Work

No More)

*C*onsidering the lyric content of *Yo! MTV Raps*, it's hard to imagine there was once a legendary fifties do-wop deemed too low-down, nasty, and degrading to be played on R & B radio. It wasn't just that the song talked about sex by euphemistically referring to it as "work." The real problem concerned Hank Ballard & the Midnighters singing about a social issue so unspeakable, so offensive to the moral fabric of Black America, so low-life ignorant and damaging to the image of the race, most R & B program directors and deejays wouldn't allow it on the airwaves.

Was it a paean to incest? Serial murder? Interracial marriage (this *was* the fifties)? None of the above. How about unmarried pregnancy:

> *Annie had a baby*
> *Can't work no more.*
> *(Do wop, do-o-o-o wop)*
> *Every time she go to work*
> *She got to get the baby off the floor.*
> *(Do wop, do-o-o-o wop)*

Think about the 1995 update. DeVon would be rapping about his woman Sheniqua who decided to give him a baby after going with him for three weeks which pissed DeVon off because even though he hadn't made a baby lately he never really liked the nappy-headed bitch so he quit her and is living off some light-skinned 'ho named Tyisha but everything's okay because Sheniqua's studying for her GED and her grandma is getting paid by the city to keep the baby as a foster child. Do wop.

The question for today is: When did wanton babymaking become more socially acceptable than picking your nose in public? At what point in the last forty years did impregnation replace conversation as a means of getting to know someone better? Was an Eleventh Commandment handed down to twelve-year-olds, stating, "Thou shalt go forth and multiply at your earliest convenience"? Was I so lost in the disco beat that I didn't notice the laws of nature being repealed? Can any of this be blamed on Murphy Brown?

I DON'T KNOW NOTHIN' 'BOUT BIRTHIN' NO BABIES

In the fifties, this is all I learned about premarital sex: No man is going to buy the cow if he can get the milk for free.

In the fifties, this is all I learned about premarital pregnancy: Heifers who calve are permanently tainted meat.

There was a decided double standard between doing it and getting caught. Sex might have been seamy, sleazy, slimy, and wrong, but nobody had to know it happened. It was your own dirty little secret, hidden in the backseat of a Chevy (or, if you were a California girl like I was, in the front seat of a sports car while trying to avoid third gear). Even good girls did it. They just acted like they didn't.

Pregnancy, on the other hand, was living proof you'd committed a crime against God, nature, humanity, Ozzie and Harriet, Mamie Eisenhower, Billy Graham, and/or the Pope. Unless your name was Mary and you'd just gotten off the boat from Bethlehem, pregnancy labeled you as damaged goods, used merchandise, round-heeled, the town pump. Oh, let's be real here: a Scarlet *S* Slut. No white wedding fantasies in your future, honey. You were going straight to hell in a handbasket, with a brief stopover at your local chapter of either the Florence Crittenden Home for Unwed Mothers or the Seven Sorrows of Our Sorrowful Mother Infants' Home. Do not pass go. Do not collect government "entitlements."

Contrary to the unique sociological theories of Senator Moynihan, these attitudes prevailed in the Black community as well as in the white. Okay, we African-Americans didn't always toss our unmarried mothers out with the afterbirth. Like all fifties Americans, though, we were mortified by their transgression. Pregnancy outside of marriage was a sign of low character. It brought shame on the family. It screamed to the world that our mothers had failed to teach us how to keep our dresses down.

IT'S A MAN THING—YOU WOULDN'T UNDERSTAND

Given the current state of barely teenaged single mothers in America, there are a whole big bunch of people who think the world was much better off when this double standard was in place. It stands to reason that a great number of people who think this way are men. (This may be the one topic on which Pat Buchanan and Louis Farrakhan could develop a dialogue.) "Double standard" meant it was woman's work to maintain the standards while guys had double the fun. It also meant that men could have their cake, eat it, and, just in case someone asked them to pay for it, go to court and swear they'd shared it with their friends, so they wouldn't have to cough up child support.

There are a lot of people who mistook this for morality, but double standards are to morality what rabid cops are to the legal system: fear and intimidation when your personal version of right and wrong just won't get the job done.

SEX AND THE SINGLE NEGRO

In actuality, the simple double standard with its one set of rules for women and a different one for men applied only to white America. Black Americans were juggling a sexual standard with so many more complex, conflicting, and irrational mores and myths, it's no wonder it finally came crashing down with the impact of the asteroid that killed the dinosaurs.

To outsiders (particularly "normal" Americans, Gingrichly speaking), it probably *appeared* that African-Americans had a less constricted attitude toward sex. I'll admit we sometimes dressed a little more flamboyantly than Beaver Cleaver's mother. There was that genetically inherited jungle-rhythm thing in our dance steps. But just because we didn't seem like we were uptight sexually didn't mean we didn't bring our own convoluted brand of weirdness to the issue.

Black women have always had a contradictory relationship with sex and sexuality, but what else would you expect from a group once looked on as pagan, wild-hipped sirens who lured virtuous slave masters away from their God-fearing spouses and introduced them to savage love rituals? Sisters were apparently so uninhibited, we didn't mind parading our bared breasts through the pages of *National Geographic* and inspiring the sexual fantasies of generations of prepubescent white boys. While Doris Day two-stepped, we shook our moneymaker. We'd go to church on Sunday and cabaret all night Monday. We were loose-living, loose-loving, good-time gals, according to the myth.

At the same time, we were also the women who never really recovered from the psychological abuse of rape during slavery (if fear wasn't passed down through our genes, it certainly came through our mothers). We had to fight off white men who assumed they were our idea of a hot time; fight four hundred years of ingrained— and often sexist—Christian morality (as interpreted by our slave owners to keep us in our place); fight off the African and Muslim traditions of defining women as less valued than the sons they produce; fight off too many years of believing in our own, occasionally self-inflicted, mythology. Plus, we based much of our self-image on Black men who openly admitted their real fantasy was white women because we were "too uptight." Like we were supposed to be able to make sense out of all this.

Not that Black men were having a better time of it. They were known as "studs." Bulls. Bush-whacking, womb-whomping, pile-driving love machines. But it's hard having your entire self-image based on the one part of your anatomy most likely to go soft. Particularly when every other societal definition of manhood and basic humanity is denied you, including power over your own destiny and the ability to provide for and protect your family.

WHY DON'T WE DO IT IN THE ROAD

As if history hadn't left us confused enough, the sixties threw a sexual revolution into the mix. To add a personal note, I know exactly what this meant to me as a teenager: no more blue-balled boyfriends and twitches in parts of my anatomy I didn't know existed. When I got my first packet of birth-control pills, the still-experimental ones with so much estrogen your breasts tripled in size overnight and life became an everlasting PMS attack, a friend claims she found me hollering, "Free at last." I do not remember this happening, but it sounds fairly reasonable.

Still, the sexual revolution from the way I remember it, from the corner of Haight and Ashbury during the summer of '67, had nothing to do with getting pregnant. It had a lot to do with sex. Protected sex. Birth-controlled sex. Okay, I'll admit it, *never, ever* condom sex, but you better believe there was always something standing in the way of Ms. Egg and Mr. Sperm getting to know each other better. At least that was the game plan.

Of course there were a few women *choosing* to bring a love child into the world while Diana Ross sang their theme song. The rest of us, though, were much more interested in feeling groovy and finding ourselves while doing our own thing by any means necessary. We knew the *real* meaning of pro-life: A woman should have a life before she brings another one into the world. We had the good sense to be aware that unrestrained egocentrism and parenting are not often a good mix. Besides, babies had to be taken care of. They required that the person giving birth act responsibly, and who in their right mind wanted to do that?

BIRTH CONTROL IS GENOCIDE OR WHY I HAD MY BABY FOR THE BLACK REVOLUTION

Many of you may remember that Stokely Carmichael once said the only position for a woman in the movement is prone (I know *I'll* never forget). I hate to say the revolutionary brothers were chauvinists, but I do recall Ron Karenga, the founder of Kwanzaa, requiring his women to walk three paces behind him (perhaps this is why they were called followers and he got to be the leader). Bobby Seale once screamed at me that I didn't know my place. The problem was that I did, and he didn't.

Sexual freedom met with a mixed reaction in this segment of the community. Yeah, it was great that the sisters felt free to *do it*, but brothers' identities depended on the idea that women were subservient while men made all the big decisions. If we were going to pose a united front, after all, *somebody* had to be in charge. Besides, sexually free women might become intellectually free women, asking too many questions about the fact that they were not allowed to ask questions, and that would certainly not be good for the race. In fact, some brothers had hard-copy proof that feminism was created solely as a divide-and-conquer tactic by whitey to make Black men feel inadequate and to sidetrack them from the serious task of nation building. It was probably a J. Edgar Hoover operation.

Fortunately, the brothers happened upon the same solution returning World War II GIs used to put Rosie the Riveter back in her place: a 1967 update of barefoot-and-pregnant called "it's your job to have a baby for the revolution." If it's nation-building time, the best way to get strong Black warriors is to create them from scratch. As many as possible, as quickly as possible. Baby-making was a revolutionary act against the system, not to mention your civic duty. (Just try not to think about how you're going to have to support little Nkrumah Malik, since his father is too busy creating a new world to be bothered with sending you a check.)

When abortion was legalized soon after this time, the same brothers went back to these same arguments for many of the same reasons:

"How can you consider an abortion when we're trying to build a nation and we need all the bodies we can get?"

"How can you consider an abortion when you know the white man is systematically trying to wipe us off the face of the earth?"

"How can you consider killing *my* baby, and why is the white man giving you permission to make this decision without my consent?"

Abortion must be genocide.

IF GOD HAD WANTED SEX EDUCATION TAUGHT IN SCHOOL, HE WOULD HAVE SAID SO IN THE BIBLE

Sexual revolutions and abortions on demand also took their toll on traditional voices of authority. Most men felt a loss of power. Women whose dreams were limited to a nice guy who'd work eight hours a day and let them stay home to cook, clean, and mother felt threatened. Churches, whose raison d'être included establishing moral parameters, felt threatened. Conservatives felt threatened. Even plenty of middle-of-the-roaders thought things had gone too far. It was time to take back the country before

Sodom and Gomorrah veered any farther into Beelzebubville.

So how do you stop kids from having sex? Not a problem. Remove sex education from the schools and they won't have to think about it.

How do you stop abortions after they've been declared a constitutional right by the Supreme Court? Not a problem. Just start a massive, incredibly well-financed PR campaign that defines you as pro-life and the opposition as pro-murder. This may have a slightly disturbing effect on intelligent, independent-minded adult women, but it will have a profound effect on teenagers who already feel guilty for having had sex in the first place. They'll be afraid not to bring to term the pregnancies they didn't want but didn't know how to prevent because they had no access to birth-control information. We couldn't legislate abstinence, so we provided fear and guilt. God's in His heaven; all's right with the world.

WHY SHENIQUA HAD A BABY

Here's how the messages of the last forty years got filtered down to Sheniqua:

Good girls don't have sex, but it's fun to have sex, so go ahead and do it, but don't use birth control, because that would be admitting you planned to have sex (which good girls don't). And once you get pregnant (which you will), don't have an abortion, because it's part of the white man's plot against your people and your man, and besides, God says if you play, you pay. That's the way He and Nancy Reagan planned it.

And you wonder why we have a social problem.

I keep reading about how Black *men* are at risk, because the odds say they have a good chance of ending up dead or incarcerated before the age of twenty-one. Like having a baby at thirteen isn't the same thing. Like taking on motherhood when you've got no support, no education, no skills, no home of your own, no income, and no hope for an improved future isn't tantamount to being buried alive.

I guess this is one of the points where this book stops being funny.

AMERICA

The Board

Game

BACKGROUND

The year is 1981. Some people claim it's morning in America, but to you it looks like high noon. The Forces of Evil are amassing in their oval-shaped headquarters, ready to turn back the clock to the glory days when Rock Hudson was a sex symbol, Pat Boone was a rock star, Norman Vincent Peale was the only self-help guru, Donna Reed wore spike heels while vacuuming, all religions were Christian, and, according to the enemy's telegenic but slightly vacant leader, *nobody* knew racism existed.

You are facing a daunting challenge. Your opponents have Congress, the Justice Department, the press, and, according to rumor, God on their side. All you have is a job obtained through affirmative action and a two-bedroom home bought with a HUD loan. The odds, not to mention history, are against you, but this may be your last chance to beat the enemy at its own game.

Are you up to the challenge? Can you fight the world's most daunting public-relations machine without protection from the Justice Department? Can you stop a legislative steamroller without support from either the media or public opinion? Does it bother you that even if you win, you'll probably end up a loser? If your response is, Hey, that's the way things go in AMERICA [:the Board Game], then get ready to play!

Number of Players

If there are only two players, one plays a single black marker while the other plays nine white markers. No matter the number of players, there should always be nine white markers for every one black marker on the board in order to keep the odds even.

Equipment

> 10 black markers, 90 white markers
> 1 pair loaded dice
> $4 trillion in unmarked bills
> Just My Luck cards
> Fat Chance cards

One board with a fifty-square perimeter, which is clearly separated from a large inner-city square by white picket fences topped with barbed wire. Outer squares are called Wall Street, Rodeo Drive, Park Avenue, Lakeshore Drive, and so on. The inner square is surrounded by an eight-lane highway named Dr. Martin Luther King, Jr., Boulevard, which has no exits to the outer squares. (There is also a thin, grayish, dying area called Middle America between the inner and outer squares. Although it is affected by everything that happens in the game, and players pay lip service to it, it can be treated as if it is not there.)

Object of the Game

The primary goal of black-marker players is to stay in place without losing ground. Their other goal is to avoid landing in the inner-city square, which operates like a roach motel: You can get in, but you can't get out. If this occurs, black-marker players automatically forfeit.

The goal of white-marker players is to amass as much cash as possible without being forced to share.

To Set Up

One white-marker player is designated as the banker. At the start, the banker gives out 98 percent of the cash on hand to 2 percent of the players, leaving the remainder to be fought over by everyone else. (Please note: If a black-marker player is accidentally included in the larger share, the game ends immediately.) It is the banker's job to make sure no money passes between the outer squares and the inner-city square.

If, during play, the banker needs more money, he mints it and makes a notation in the deficit column of his ledger.

To Play

To determine who goes first, the players each toss the dice; the highest number leads off. (It should be noted that because the dice are loaded, the leader will be a white-marker player under all circumstances.)

White-marker players move forward.

Black-marker players move backward.

White-marker players proceed around the board as quickly as possible, collecting cash whenever available and cheating when the opportunity arises. Since black-marker players are simply trying to stay in place, white-marker players assist them by denying them two out of three of their designated turns.

Just My Luck Cards

Randomly placed around the board are spaces requiring black-marker players to pick a card. At the top of each card is a black cat walking under a ladder, with instructions such as:

Trickle-down economy isn't trickling in your direction. Go back 3 spaces.

Your son's school lunch program calls catsup a vegetable and substitutes it for broccoli. Go back 1 space.

Deregulation means your small business can be legally bankrupted by a large conglomerate. Go back 24 spaces.

Nancy Reagan tells your drug-addicted nephew to "just say no" as her husband eliminates all drug rehabilitation programs. Go back 5 spaces.

Nancy Reagan tells your 16-year-old daughter to "just say no" as her husband's Religious Right supporters eliminate sex education and condom distribution in schools. Go back 7 spaces.

Nancy Reagan feels it's all right to tell children to "just say no," even though she got pregnant before she married Ronnie. Tell her to go to hell.

You invested your entire life savings in Silverado Savings Bank. Go back 18 spaces.

Capital-gains tax cuts mean nothing to you. Stay where you are.

Crack is moving into your neighborhood. Quit while you're ahead.

You're an air-traffic controller. The game is over.

Fat Chance Cards

Every third space is a Fat Chance space, requiring black-marker players to pick a card. At the top of each card is a picture of opportunity knocking, encased in a red circle with a line across to indicate the international symbol for *no*. Fat Chance cards include instructions like:

William Casey has opened up 300 new agent positions at the CIA. Do not bother to apply.

Drexel Burnham Lambert is issuing discount bonds guaranteed to make each holder an instant multimillionaire. Nobody bothered to tell you.

General Electric is building a factory and wants to buy up your neighborhood for pennies on the dollar. You make a plea to the President to intervene.

HUD is building 800,000 homes in your area and you're a developer. The person bidding against you for the minority contract is a cousin of Ed Meese with the surname Puffington-Lopez.

Your race- and gender-discrimination suit against the Forestry Service will be personally handled by a man named Clarence Thomas.

You file an application to prevent Interior Secretary James Watt from building a hazardous-waste dump in your child's classroom.

You ask the Justice Department to file a friend-of-the-court brief in your brutality suit against the Orange County Police Department.

You write a letter asking to have your indigent, blind, incapacitated, and homeless 107-year-old grandmother's food stamps reinstated.

You try to find out the ingredients in government cheese.

Bonus Opportunities

Anytime white-marker players land on a Phone Conversation with Ivan Boesky space, they automatically triple their cash on hand. (When black-marker players land on this space, the line goes dead.)

Penalties

If caught cheating, white-marker players must give .5 percent of their cash on hand to the charity of their choice (tax-deductible, of course).

Black-marker players caught cheating must pay full restitution plus exorbitant penalties, and serve a term in a maximum-security prison before receiving the death penalty. (This is to deter others from committing similar crimes, not for revenge.)

"Go to the Inner City" Spaces

On three corners of the board are spaces depicting a pointing finger. Underneath is the message:

Go directly to the inner city. Do not pass Go. Do not ever again collect a paycheck.

Black-marker players follow the instructions to the letter.

White-marker players are allowed to land on the outer perimeter of the space, marked Just Visiting. After performing several hours of community service, they continue the game.

To Win

In this particular edition of the game, he who has the most money when he dies wins. Everyone else has just been running around in circles, with the illusion they were part of the game.

White-marker players: If you were ahead at the beginning, you should still be ahead at the end.

Black-marker players: If you managed to stay in the game, consider yourself lucky. The rules will have to change eventually, after all. In the near future you can count on the American people getting tired of the status quo, voting the bums out, and creating an exciting and challenging new game in Washington.

We Finally Got a Piece of the Pie-ie-ie

*C*ontrary to popular opinion, the news in African America is not all bad. Yes, there have been setbacks. Okay, total reversals. Like the only difference between 1995 and Reconstruction is that Jesse Helms is not wearing white robes in public.

Be that as it may, it's important that we look at the positive side so that those of us among the less fortunate have something to strive for. In the spirit of Booker T. Washington and *Ebony* magazine, here's a list of recent accomplishments for which the Negro race can pat its collective self on the back:

Gladys Knight is the official spokesperson for Aunt Jemima.

Bobby Seale, who once believed the revolution would not be televised, does Ben & Jerry's ads.

Martin Luther King, Jr., has been designated an official shopping day.

Black conservative Republicans in Congress have not yet mentioned the words *separate*, *but*, and *equal* in the same sentence.

Malcolm X is a hat.

Bessie Smith is a stamp.

Home Boy condoms are available in jumbo sizes at chain drugstores.

Hallmark stores have an official Kwanzaa section every December.

Employees in the Harlem McDonald's wear authentic imitation kente-cloth uniforms.

You can shop for Afrocentrism in the Afrocentric boutique area at JCPenney (and charge it on your American Express, Visa, or Master-Card).

Spiegel will send you your own catalog featuring African-Americanish clothing.

Spike Lee is available at Macy's.

You don't have to search for Abraham Lincoln High School anymore if you're trying to locate the Black neighborhood in a city. Instead, you can head straight for Martin Luther King, Jr., Boulevard.

We Are Overcome

Why Martin Luther King, Jr., Needed a Jheri Curl and a Better Theme Song

*I*t must have been 1981 or 1982 when I got off a plane at LAX, looked around the airport, and got slapped in the face with a *hairstyle*. To the left and to the right of me, from the powerplayers to the players, from the baggage handlers to the panhandlers, every last Black male crossing my sight lines had a head full of slime-dripping, glow-in-the-daylight, never-lay-next-to-nature, jerry-built, Jheri-curled, high-octane ringlets clinging pitifully to his pimply, glistening forehead.

Had someone forgotten to tell me there'd been a run on Pennzoiled pubic-hair transplants to relieve male-pattern baldness? Were they all entering a Curly the Stooge lookalike contest? Had they had some prescient mass vision of Samuel L. Jackson in *Pulp Fiction* and thought he looked like he grew it himself? Was I not privy to a collective decision to replace ritual scarification with tonsorial mutilation as a neo-African rite of passage?

It was almost as if *G.Q.* had declared it de rigueur for Black males to resemble Valvoline-dipped Pre-Raphaelite poodles. Or as if some alien force had seeded the South Central clouds with a brain-eating curl activator, inducing a zombielike state that caused the victims not to realize they were slathering their hair with a caustic substance closely akin to Drano, twisting it around pink curlers, sticking it in a plastic bag, and topping off the finished product with a twelve-ounce can of Pam cooking spray.

What was clear was that these mis-tressed, distressed males, who not so many years before would have been proclaiming the depth of their Blackness with the height of their Afro, were no longer identifying with the Kunta Kintenicity of their natural roots. Somehow, a deeply suppressed, unarticulated aching for the ultimate counter-Afrocentric fantasy, *blowin'-in-the-wind hair*, had reared its ugly head.

All societies reveal their collective psyche through external cultural signs, and for Black America, hair has consistently been a primary gauge of self-identity and self-esteem. African-American hair is one of those things that traditionally did not melt down in the melting pot, no matter how much heat was applied. In actuality, it frequently had a short, nappy little mind of its own that refused to conform to this country's premulticultural vision of a standard model all-American.

Within the African-American race, hair has often had a direct bearing on social status (meaning that there were always those groups of Blacks who didn't want you to marry into their families if you couldn't grow any). The theory held that flowing, kinkless hair was infinitely more attractive than a short crop of beadlets that presented too much of an African motif. Of course, the natural presence of "blow hair" on your head probably meant that one of your female ancestors had been brutally raped by a slave master, but that is a fact that, for many historical and misogynistic reasons, has been frequently interpreted as an advantage by the Black community.

Within the African-American race, the choice of hairstyle has also always been a covert indicator of the emotional well-being of its bearer. The question is not one of whether hair is worn natural or chemically altered. It has more to do with whether maintenance of the particular style of choice:

1. takes an average of three hours a day, not including interim fluff-ups;
2. necessitates spending more than the annual gross national product of Grenada in the ethnic hair-care section of the drugstore; or . . .
3. involves sleeping in a stocking cap, do-rag, grease-filled Baggie, or any other headpiece capable of causing profound embarrassment if a fire broke out in the middle of the night and you were spied by the neighbors.

Clearly the Jheri-curled eyesores infesting L.A. and the rest of the country in the early eighties met all of the above criteria. This was particularly disconcerting, since barely a decade previously most African-Americans (except, perhaps, Diana Ross) decided that "Black is Beautiful" meant accepting their natural kinkiness. Yet in the amount of time it took for disco to come and go, "Black is Beautiful" had turned into "Black is lyed, dyed, fried, and blow-dried." James Brown had beat out the Afroed-centric prototype in the tressed-for-success role-model sweepstakes.

I couldn't blame what was happening on the Reagan years, because they hadn't been invented yet. It wasn't inspired by MTV videos, because, in the early eighties, MTV still hadn't decided if racial integration was part of its marketing plan. It couldn't be laid at the feet of commercial television, since, in that pre-Cosby era, just about the only Black image on the networks was Mr. T (who also could be counted among the hairdo-impaired, but not in a way that would inspire mass emulation).

Many of the people who currently influence African-American mass culture were otherwise engaged. Louis Farrakhan was just another reincarnated calypso singer trying to reach a mass market by any means necessary ("any means," according to most Black Nationalists at the time, included ordering the death of Malcolm X). Ron Karenga, the creator of Kwanzaa, was recovering from his Rick James phase after serving hard time for savagely and sadistically torturing a woman as she lay chained in his basement for several days. The Reverend Al Sharpton was busy with his FBI informant activities. Ice Cube, Ice T, Dr. Dre, and the rest of the rappers hadn't yet turned in their gang-banging credentials to become capitalists.

I simply couldn't find a logical reason why a large segment of an entire race would choose to look like Little Orphan Annie OD'd on Brylcreem, but I wasn't the only one confused. The CEO of the largest Black-owned hair-care company would not let his marketing staff develop a Jheri curl–like product because he was certain the Black community would not be dumb enough to commit hair-related hara-kiri. Since this decision almost sunk his business, obviously he was wrong. I had agreed with him, and I was wrong. What neither of us realized was that something was seriously *wack* in Black America.

Maybe I'm just imagining things, but I don't think we acted this way before integration. When African-Americans were legally (or psychologically) restricted to living among themselves, there wasn't much tolerance for anyone who walked around embarrassing the race. A people who've seen themselves defined only in negative images do not like to have those stereotypes reinforced. Not to mention that God don't like ugly. So before integration, any African-American male hanging out in the neighborhood with hair resembling a furry animal caught in the Exxon *Valdez* spill would have had the "Black" laughed out of him. This is a fact.

When it came to anything attracting inordinate attention, the basic attitude was: White folks may do that, but *we* don't. This was a defense mechanism created by a people who'd spent four hundred years trying not to call too much attention to themselves. Maybe it had something to do with fear of being beaten, raped, lynched, castrated, unjustly incarcerated, or, at the very least, generically disrespected, but it covered everything from walking outside with your hair uncombed to serial killing. This attitude included both moral superiority and moral certainty—a sense that no matter how bad things got within the race, we were always going to hold ourselves better than *them*.

Maintaining moral superiority was easy when racism slapped you in the face with its WHITES ONLY signs. If you were an African-American, you had never lynched an innocent man, and neither had your friends or relatives. (Of course, a lot of white folks hadn't either, but they weren't the ones who counted.) You had not aimed attack dogs and high-powered fire hoses at children. You had not blown little girls into heaven while they sat praying in church. Above all, no matter what you had done in your life as an African-American, you had not wrenched millions of people from their homeland, stuffed them—chained—into the steaming, putrid holds of ships, and brought them to an alien nation, where they were bred and sold like cattle. You were secure in the fact that you'd always be totally and everlastingly morally superior to *that*, if nothing else.

By the seventies, though, this sense of moral

superiority began to get murky. The certainty that guided people through four hundred years of slavery and its aftermath and the moral focal points against which right and wrong had always been measured were beginning to unravel. People began asking too many questions, such as:

Why are the Panthers partying at Leonard Bernstein's house instead of saving the world from democracy?

Why am I paying rent to a ghetto slumlord when I could be blockbusting the suburbs?

Will a poor-but-pure revolutionary get to heaven faster than a rich-but-happy, affirmative-actioned capitalist-in-training? As a follow-up: Does it matter if my Afro won't fit through the eye of a needle?

If the Nation of Islam's Elijah Muhammad made women cover their bodies to protect them from men, who was protecting them from Elijah Muhammad?

Should I stick to my principles and force my boss to accept my dashiki, or would I look more irresistible in Tiffany cuff links?

Am I betraying the race if I buy a Bee Gees album?

Being that this was twenty-something years before LaToya's psychic hot line, nobody had the answers.

The civil rights movement had had some tangible effects. *In-your-face* segregation gave way to redlined neighborhoods, glass ceilings, and last hired/first-fired affirmative-action programs. Racism was no longer law, but just another part of the decision-making process. Inevitably, some African-Americans began to believe they were finally being mainstreamed. For them, the larger world took on more meaning and the Black community ceased to be their primary point of reference.

Unfortunately, Head Start was not created soon enough to help everyone make the jump to integration. While the upwardly mobile were trying to get a piece of the pie and expatriates from the civil rights movement were trying to get a piece of the War on Poverty, African-Americans who couldn't escape were singing their own tune:

> *Keeping your head above water.*
> *Making it any way you can.*
> *Temporary layoffs.*
> *(Good times!)*
> *Easy Credit rip-offs.*
> *(Good times!)*
> *Ain't we lucky we got 'em?*
> *Good times!*

No leadership, no jobs, no money, and no way to get any of the above. A vacuum had been created in the Black community, and Hollywood was there to fill it.

By the early seventies, the film industry was in a financial bind, mainly because it had continued to make silly, sexist, exclusionary, escapist films long after reality dictated that the world had gone on to bigger and better things. Box-office receipts reached a historic low and many of the major studios were on the verge of collapse. Into the void came an idea to make films for the African-American audience—films with no perceivable scripts, no production values, and no redeeming social value. They all had an identical plot:

FADE IN.

A big Black man dressed in more leather than a Porsche interior and three-inch platform shoes enters. He is larger than life (with a gun and a dick to match) and speaks fluent ghetto. To the beat of a top-of-the-charts sound track (you know how much they love to dance), he wipes out all the dope dealers in the major urban area of your choice without getting a drop of blood on his bell-bottoms. Then he makes love to the (most loyal, foxiest, chestiest) member of his harem.

FADE OUT.

For African-American children raised on the concept of Black Power without having had a chance to see anyone exercise it, the Black Macho Man packing ten pounds of steel in his holster and ten inches of solid gold between his legs became the penultimate hero. Like every Black man worth looking up to historically, he remained an outlaw, even when he worked for the law (and "he" was occasionally a "she," like Pam Grier, which didn't make the image any less macho).

There was empowerment in this solitary, monosyllabic, wandering man with his wandering penis. He demonstrated the possibilities of what could happen if a righteous brother ignored the rules and took matters into his own hands. Straddling the thin line between freedom and anarchy, only *he* could help the morally upright, hardworking-but-naïve ghettoites rid the community of drugs. Only *he* could kill the corrupt cops and let the pitiful, ravaged, positively thinking, Black-consciously aware former Negroes return to building the Umoja community center and raise their children to be righteous brothers and sisters. So what if he was vicious, violent, arrogant, and treated all women like sluts? At least when he was done with you, you knew you'd been fucked.

The impact of these images on an entire generation cannot be underestimated. In a world without focus and direction, anyone with a map is a hero, no matter where the roads lead. There were no other threats to the authority of these images. Malcolm X was dead. Martin Luther King, Jr., was dead. The civil rights movement had been buried alive.

Even if everyone had been around, it's doubtful they could have competed with the Macho Men. Malcolm and Martin had not considered the acquisition of obscene amounts of capital an inalienable right and a primary goal, making them seem naïve and altruistic. Neither Malcolm nor Martin hung out in the 'hood with fine bitches dressed in leather hot pants. Neither of them had their own theme song (okay, "We Shall Overcome," but you couldn't dance to it).

The remaining anointed Black leadership looked askance at the screen images who were replacing them as role models. They did not take kindly to this alternative to their moral authority to determine moral authority. Unfortunately, the nabobs of negritude were so busy attacking the Macho Man image, they forgot to propose an alternative vision. They also forgot that people who can't find a way to survive will identify with someone who can.

It didn't matter that the story lines of these films were unrealistic and untranslatable to real life. What was real to the believers was the knowledge that the world was perilous and drug-ridden, controlled by forces outside of the community, and salvageable only by someone who accepted this reality and moved outside the law. The values for the next generation were being set in motion.

Television offered alternative-image programming with *Roots*, but seven nights of slavery and subjugation inspired anger rather than healing—particularly when *Roots* aired while the country was undergoing phase one of a "white backlash" to the civil rights movement. It seems as if white America didn't care about equal opportunity once inflation was rampant and interest rates were climbing to an inconceivable 21 percent. They didn't care for affirmative action after realizing that when a Black person is hired, there's one less opportunity available for themselves and their friends. Not to mention the impact of the women's movement, which made white males feel doubly encroached upon.

Life went downhill quickly for the backlashed. The Supreme Court's Bakke decision came through and determined white males could be an oppressed people just like the rest of us. The ACLU supported the Klan's right to demonstrate. Black males were becoming less of a threat, since, according to FBI statistics, they had only a three-in-five chance of reaching the age of twenty-five. Cocaine was decimating the masses through freebasing. Poverty programs were dismantled. Leftover radicals were slowly, but surely, incarcerated and/or annihilated. The only revolutionary left in the country was William

Randolph Hearst's granddaughter. It was definitely not a good time to be a person of color.

Inevitably, the white backlash turned into an African-American whiplash. By the beginning of the eighties, everyone on the wrong side of the burgeoning schism between the Black middle class and the inner city was in economic decline, and destined to continue to be so. Too many Blacks, with a convoluted nationalism accented by a leftover dash of sixties paranoia, believed that everything in their world was out of their control. Too many Blacks, the ones who'd memorized every line in *Superfly*, felt that given the circumstances under which they were living, anything could be justified.

"By any means necessary" took on a new and patently dangerous meaning. Destroying your neighborhood by filling it with drugs was acceptable if that's what it took to put a dollar in your pocket. Drive-by shootings could be justified if that's what you needed to protect your turf. Giving birth at fourteen could be justified if that's what it took to keep your man coming around for another couple of months.

Logic became so convoluted, life became so disoriented, it was enough to make you grow your hair long, process it with lye, set it in a greasy, curly hairstyle, and think you looked as natural as a white boy.

And that's one of the things that went wrong with Black America.

After Words

*Y*ou may have noticed that this book has not
mentioned the O. J. Simpson murder trial.
There were no reminiscences on what I
was doing at the exact moment I first heard news
of the deaths that launched thousands of hours of
TV coverage. I did not speculate about who,
what, when, where, why, how, or, for that matter,
which specific duties define Kato Kaelin's job
description. I did not choose to share with you
which member of either the prosecution or
defense team, if any, I have embraced as my personal role model and/or savior.

This was not an accident. Even though the
media kept referring to the Simpson proceedings
as "the trial of the century," some of us in America felt, in our heart of hearts, that the gruesome
coda to a misbegotten marriage between a dyslexic

former-jock-'n-the-hood sportscaster/actor and his own private Clairol-kissed Malibu Barbie did not merit gavel-to-gavel, wall-to-wall, month-to-month national television coverage. Try as we might, there were some of us in America who were just not smart enough to find meaning in the morass.

There's only one way this trial could have had truly *national* significance, but I'm sure Oliver Stone has already verified the whereabouts of Bill Clinton on the evening of June 12, 1994, between the hours of 10:15 and 10:45. Not that it can be proved Mr. Clinton even knew Mrs. Simpson, although you must admit that she bore a distant, blondish resemblance to Jenifer Flowers. We shouldn't forget, though, that Bobby Kennedy was lying through his Bucky Beavers when he claimed he wasn't in Los Angeles on the day Marilyn Monroe "committed suicide." Unless some plucky journalist gets access to the Secret Service files through a Freedom of Information Act request, we may never know what the real deal was.

On the other hand, there is something I do know. While most of the country was riveted on O. J., there was a much more significant trial taking place on Long Island. Colin Ferguson, a man who killed six people and wounded nineteen while marching up the aisle of a commuter train demonstrating his right to bear arms, was facing a jury of his peers (if such a thing exists). Mr. Ferguson claimed, despite dozens of eyewitnesses to the contrary, that he was actually asleep when the mayhem occurred. Mr. Ferguson claimed someone stole his gun while he just wasn't looking, and this particular someone committed mass murder without once breaking into Mr. Ferguson's nap. Mr. Ferguson felt various government agencies had conspired to let this criminal go free because the real perpetrator was white, while Mr. Ferguson was not. It's a thought.

It had occurred to Mr. Ferguson's legal advisers to plead him not guilty by reason of insanity. Their client, however, refused to allow anyone to imply he was insane. Possibly because it wouldn't look good on either his permanent record or a future résumé, a reasonable attitude coming from a man out of touch with reason.

The judge could have taken the matter out of Mr. Ferguson's hands by simply declaring him insane. Except that in a society which is resentful of "criminal coddling," a society which doesn't feel safe on its own streets, in its own homes, or, now, on the Long Island Railroad, a society which wants someone, *anyone*, to pay for the fact that things are just not what they were in the good old days, the judge had to go with the only politically acceptable decision: Colin Ferguson was declared sane. Sane enough to be *punished* for his crime. Sane enough to act as his own defense attorney.

So while the rest of the world was lost in the

muddle of the O. J. trial with its multimillion-dollar prosecution budget and its multimillion-dollar defense team, on a nightly basis New York news viewers were treated to a lone apparent-madman, wearing his one, fraying suit and relying on a courtroom technique that could only have been learned from *Perry Mason* reruns. When the murder weapon was introduced, Ferguson stared trancelike and asked longingly, without taking his eyes from the gun, "May I touch the evidence?" He spoke of himself in the third person and reacted in disbelief each time a witness proclaimed, "*You* are the one who aimed your gun and shot me." *The Twilight Zone* would have rejected this script as unbelievable. But in America, 1995, a place where we're mad as hell and we're not going to take it anymore, where last year's Republican contract says there will no longer be any such thing as a free lunch or a free ride (as if anyone had been getting either), it seemed in keeping with the times.

Lately, I've been wondering if each of us in this country has more in common with Colin Ferguson than we'd care to lay claim to. We are all ready to admit that somewhere, America took a wrong-way detour on the road to life, liberty, and the pursuit of happiness. We are all aware that something got terribly botched and things fell apart. But we go to bed each night knowing, as surely as Colin Ferguson knows, that whatever bad acts were committed, *we* weren't the perpetrators.

So who did it? you may well ask. Oh, come on, the answer is obvious: *They* did it. Not only do *they* always do it, *they* always get away with it. If you don't believe me, read the *National Enquirer*. Or the *Wall Street Journal*. Or *Vibe*. And as long as each of us, regardless of race, creed, color, or gender of origin, holds on to that belief, our national dialogue will continue to sound like babbling madmen fraying at the edges, lacking rational judgment, denying reality, and, inevitably, signifying nothing.

Is there a solution? Maybe, just maybe. As a special favor, I would personally like to ask Judge Lance Ito to declare each and every citizen of the United States not guilty of past crimes by reason of insanity. I think at this juncture in his judiciary/media career, he has the power. Besides, it would be a nice gesture on his part. Then we can all start with a fresh slate on a level playing field and take personal responsibility for every single thing that happens in our lives.

Or, we can always go back to sleep and hope that nobody steals our weapons while we're not paying attention, and hope that we don't spend the rest of our lives paying for acts we can't remember committing.

(continued from front flap)

on a first-come, first-served basis, and black Americans didn't anticipate that prisons would become synonymous for low-income housing for their children. Maybe that's one reason why we all can't get along.

Bonnie Allen doesn't have *all* the answers, but she is fearless about asking the tough questions and letting the blame fall where it may (even though she knows this means, in Washington, it will fall on deaf ears). Whatever your political persuasion, race, creed, or gender of origin, you can count on one thing: She's going to leave you with a new perspective on Truth, Justice, and the American Way.

BONNIE ALLEN has written for numerous magazines and is a nationally published film and television critic. She lives with her daughter, Paloma Allen-Davis, in New York City, and thanks for their support her fellow faculty members at Peaches' School of Charm and Negro Improvement (you know who you are).